First Shape Book

KINGFISHER

KINGFISHER
Kingfisher Publications Plc
New Penderel House
283–288 High Holborn
London WC1V 7HZ
www.kingfisherpub.com

First published by Kingfisher Publications Plc 2002
2 4 6 8 10 9 7 5 3 1

1RD/0302/TIMS/FR(FR)/115OMA

A CIP catalogue record for this book is available from the British Library.

ISBN 0 7534 0670 5

Printed in China

Written by Ann Montague-Smith
Illustrated by Mandy Stanley

Editor: Jennie Morris
Designer: Jane Buckley
DTP Manager: Nicky Studdart
Production: Jo Blackmore

Contents

Suggestions for parents

Children soon learn that there are shapes all around them, but at first they cannot distinguish between the different shapes that they see. Learning about shapes – their names, characteristics, and the similarities and differences between them – is a difficult skill to acquire. By familiarizing your child with two-dimensional shapes, this colourful and inviting book will be an invaluable aid to this process.

Very young children will enjoy browsing through the book, looking at the colourful pictures. Encourage them to talk about the shapes in the pictures, name them and ask them to find other shapes that are similar.

When you look at this book together make it an enjoyable experience. Encourage your child to talk about the shapes and name them together. Point to other shapes and encourage him or her to name these shapes too. Ask your child to describe the shapes: do they have curved or straight sides? how many sides do they have? Ask him or her to seek out other examples elsewhere in the book. Your child can compare the shapes and objects drawn on the page and match them. Encourage your child to

compare the different shapes that they see so that he or she begins to understand that, although some shapes have the same number of sides, they are not the same shape.

Learning needn't stop when the book is closed! Look at things in the home and outside together, and identify them by their shape. This book should give you plenty of ideas of what to look out for. When out shopping, for example, talk about the shapes of packages, looking for boxes with square faces or the circular ends of tubes. Your child will enjoy using his or her new knowledge when playing with toys, especially those that can be used for building. Talk together about the shapes that can be seen in the faces of building blocks. Make repeating patterns using blocks or other toys, and encourage your child to describe the pattern and say what comes next.

Above all, remember that mathematics is fun!

Ann Montague-Smith

Ann Montague-Smith, Principal Lecturer in Primary Education
University College Worcester

Meet the shapes

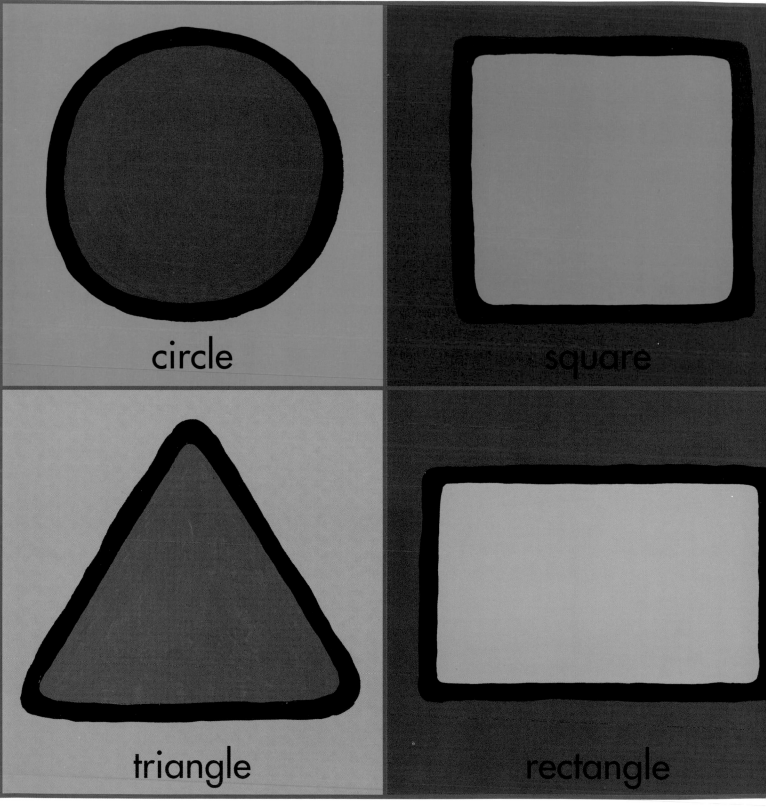

circle

square

triangle

rectangle

Which shapes are green?

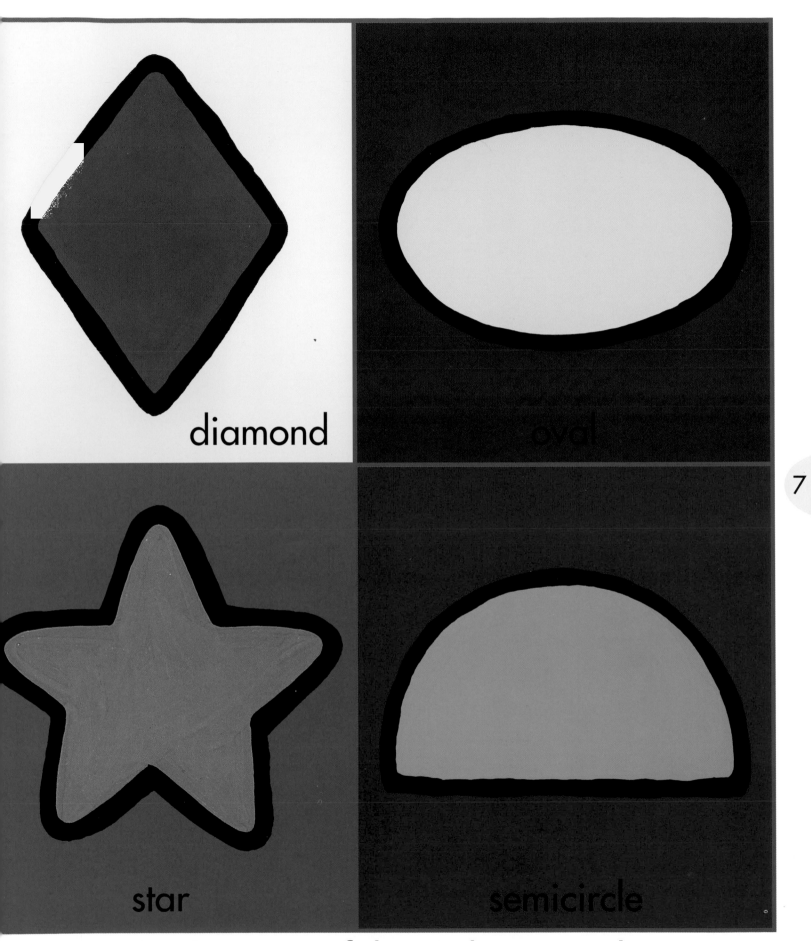

diamond

oval

star

semicircle

Can you see any of these shapes at home?

Circles

circle

rubber ring

plate

wheel

Can you draw a circle?

lolly

target board

mirror

yo-yo

paints in a palette

How many circles can you see?

Triangles

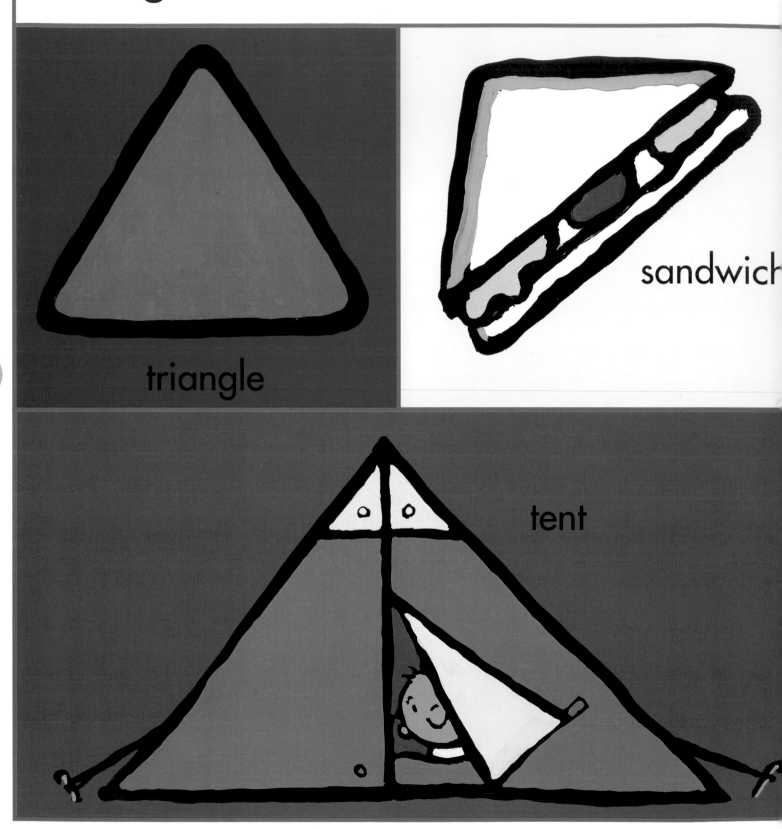

triangle

sandwich

tent

How many triangles can you count on the tent?

bunting flags

dinosaur's spikes

musical
triangle

slice of
pizza

Can you draw a triangle?

Squares

square

envelope

Mr Eric Fisher

Harbour House

Seatown

window

bag

Can you draw a square?

Come to my party

Sally

invitation

gate

1
2 3
4
5 6
7
8 9
10

hopscotch

What shape is the gate handle?

Rectangles

rectangle

A A

A A

playing card

birthday card

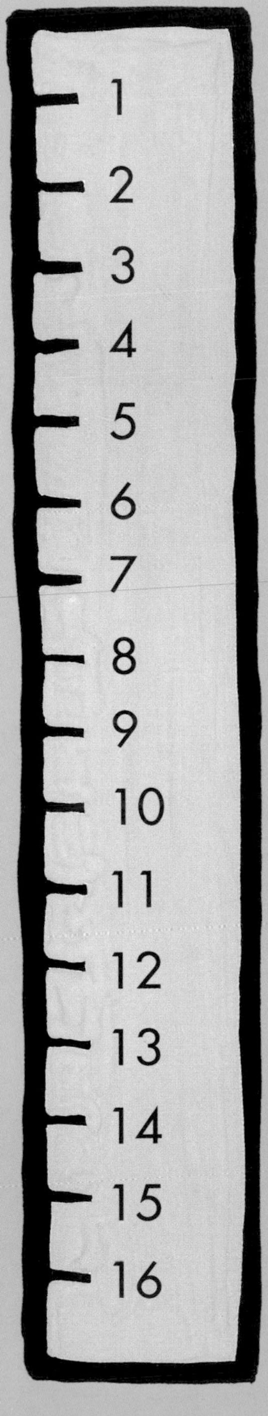

1
2
3
4
5
6
7
8
9
10
11
12
13
14
15
16

ruler

Which is the longest rectangle?

crackers

bookshelf and books

television and table

sofa and cushions

Can you see any squares?

Look again

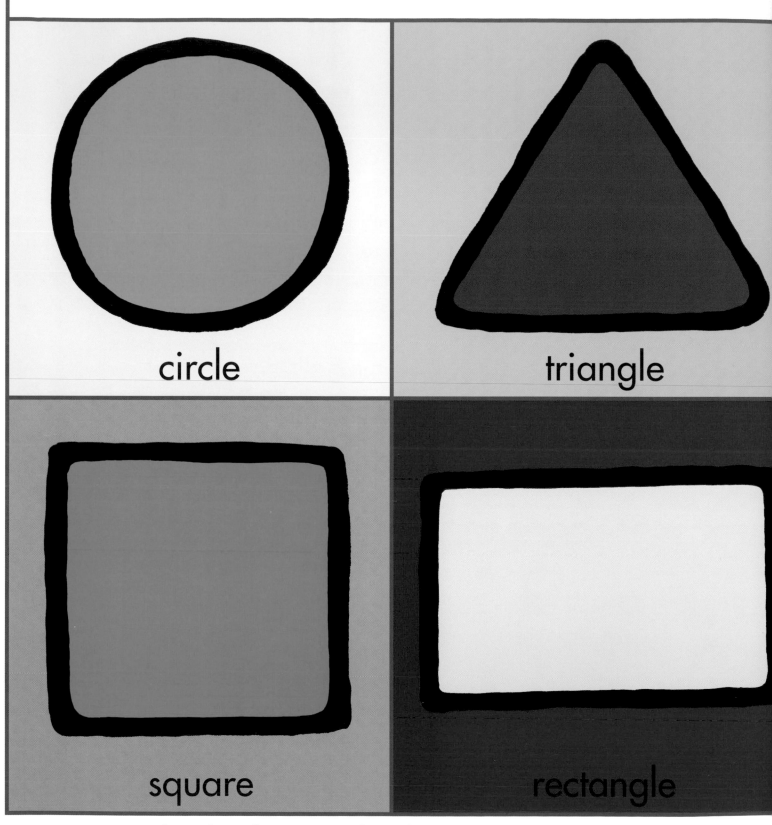

circle

triangle

square

rectangle

Which shapes look like each other?

boat

lolly

17

window

door

How many rectangles can you count?

Is it curved?

ball

banana

cat

hula
hoop

Can you trace the curves with your finger?

seahorse

gymnast

snake

apple

9

nine

Which other numbers have curves?

Is it straight?

pencil

one

see-saw

ladder

20

Which are the straight lines?

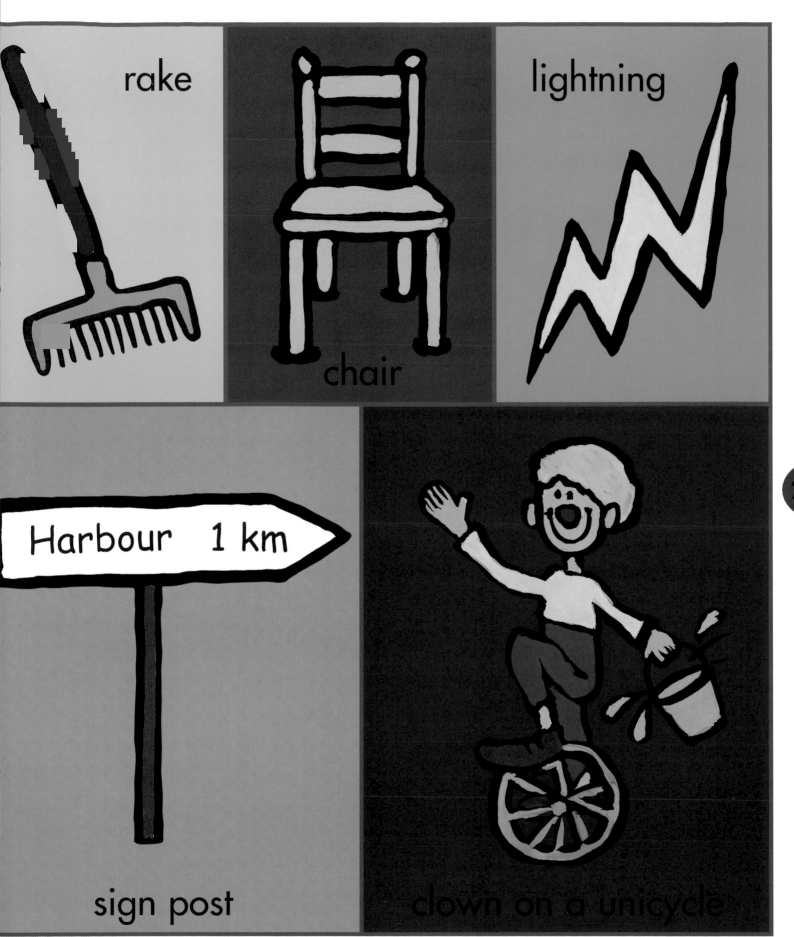

rake

chair

lightning

Harbour 1 km

sign post

clown on a unicycle

Which are the curved lines?

Stars and diamonds

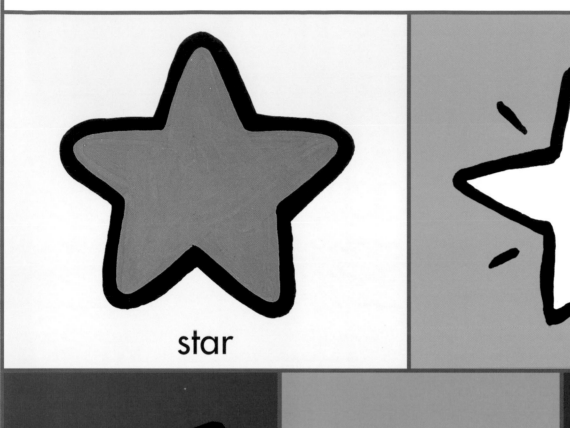

star

star

flag

starfish

fairy's wand

22

What shape is on the flag?

diamond

kite

scarf

jockey

jewels in a crown

Can you draw a kite?

Ovals

oval

picture frame

leaf

face

Can you draw an oval?

24

sink

hairbrush

pineapple

gem

zero

How many blue ovals can you see?

Circles and semicircles

lolly

cake

egg yolk

pizza

watermelon

Which circles do you like to eat?

half a lolly

half a cake

half an egg yolk

half a pizza

half a watermelon

Can you find a semicircle at home?

Match the objects to the shapes

hat

circle

rainbow

egg

rectangle

28

What shape is the egg?

semicircle

oval

ball

bag

triangle

What other things are circles?

How many sides do shapes have?

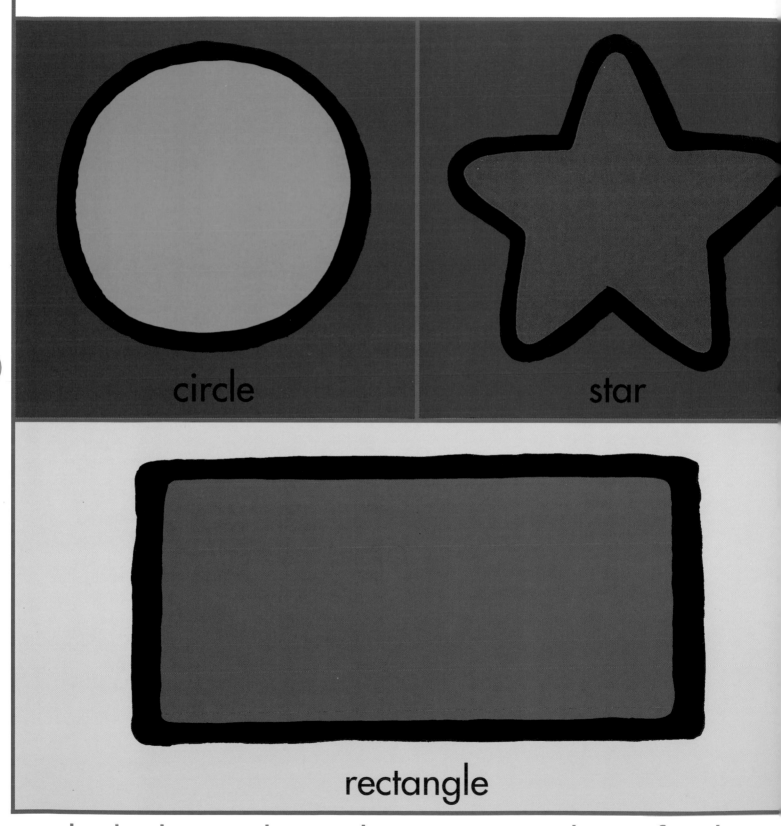

circle

star

rectangle

Which shapes have the same number of sides?

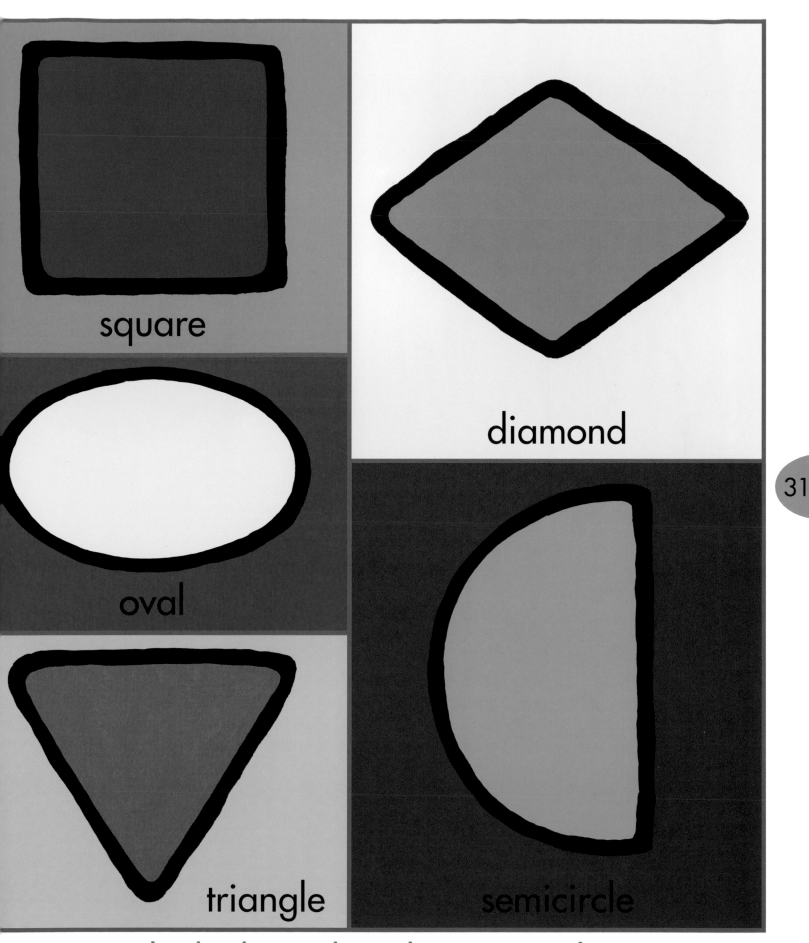

square

diamond

oval

triangle

semicircle

Which shape has the most sides?

At the playground

Which shapes have curved sides?

What other shapes can you play with?

Shapes at the seaside

flags

ice cream

beach ball

starfish

Which shapes can you see?

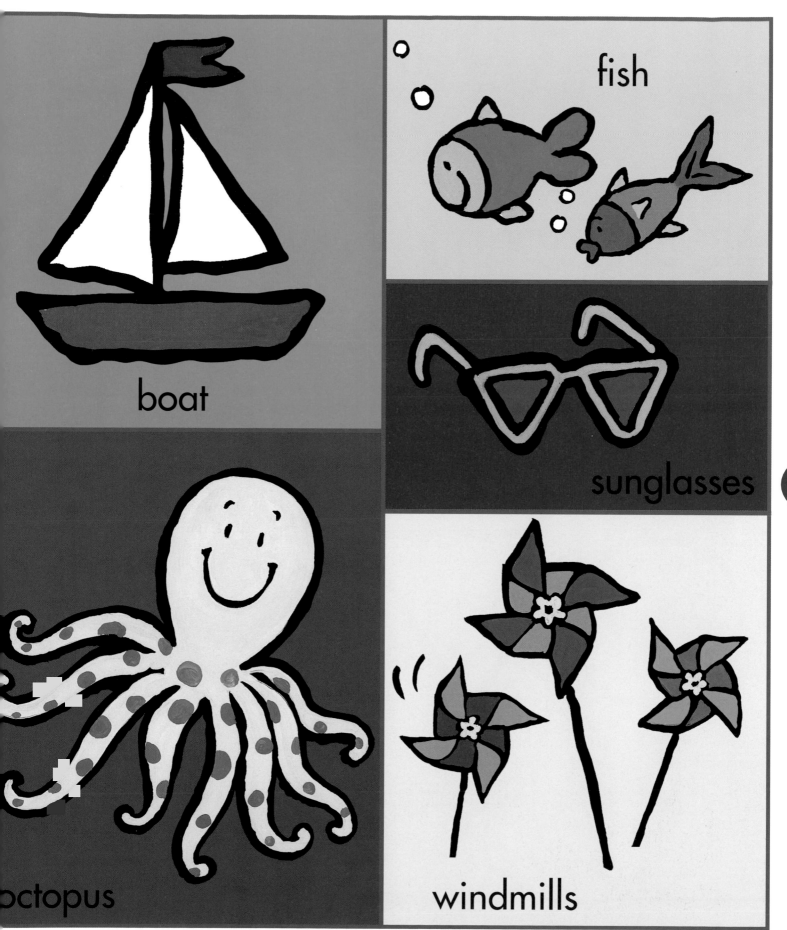

boat

fish

sunglasses

octopus

windmills

How many points does the starfish have?

Find the pairs

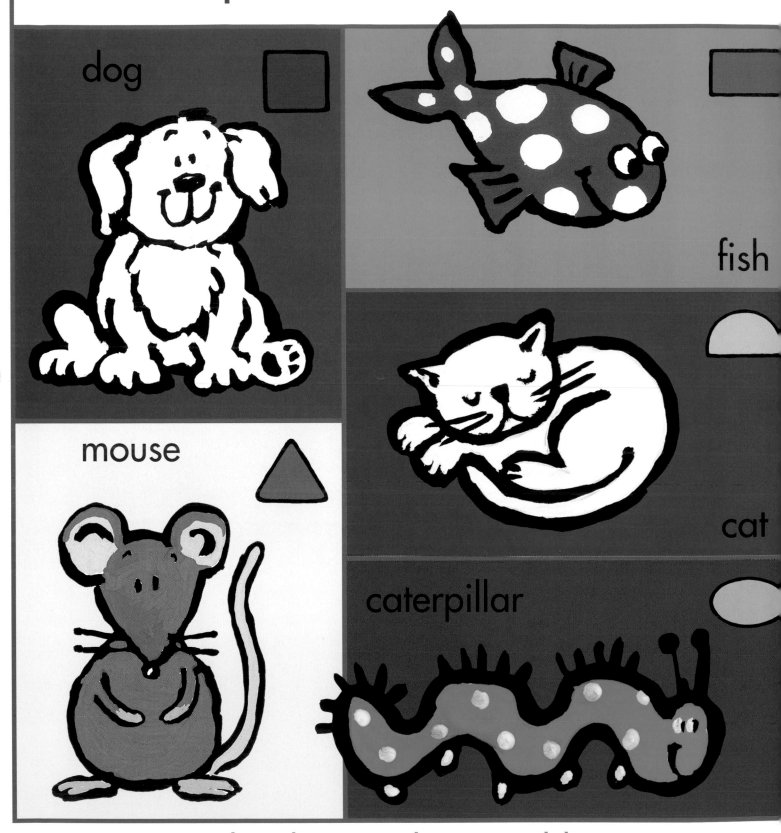

dog

fish

mouse

cat

caterpillar

36

What has each animal lost?

bed

leaf

cheese

tank

cushion

What shapes can you see in the tank?

Spot the patterns

What comes next in these patterns? And next?

Can you make up your own pattern?

Look in the mirror

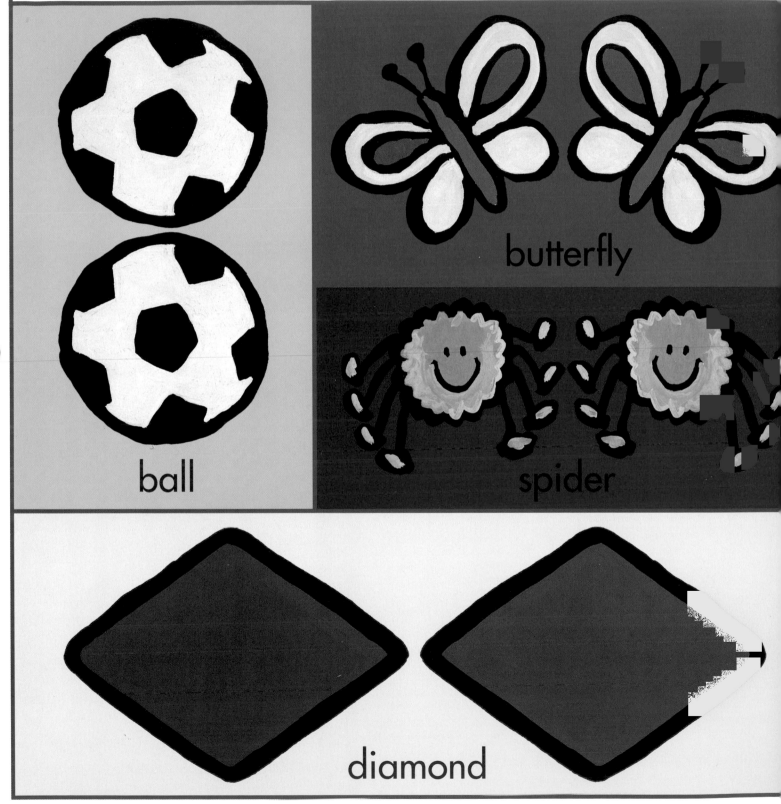

ball

butterfly

spider

diamond

Where would the mirrors be in each picture?

teddy bear

flower

puppet

eight

car

What do you see when you look in the mirror?

Big and small

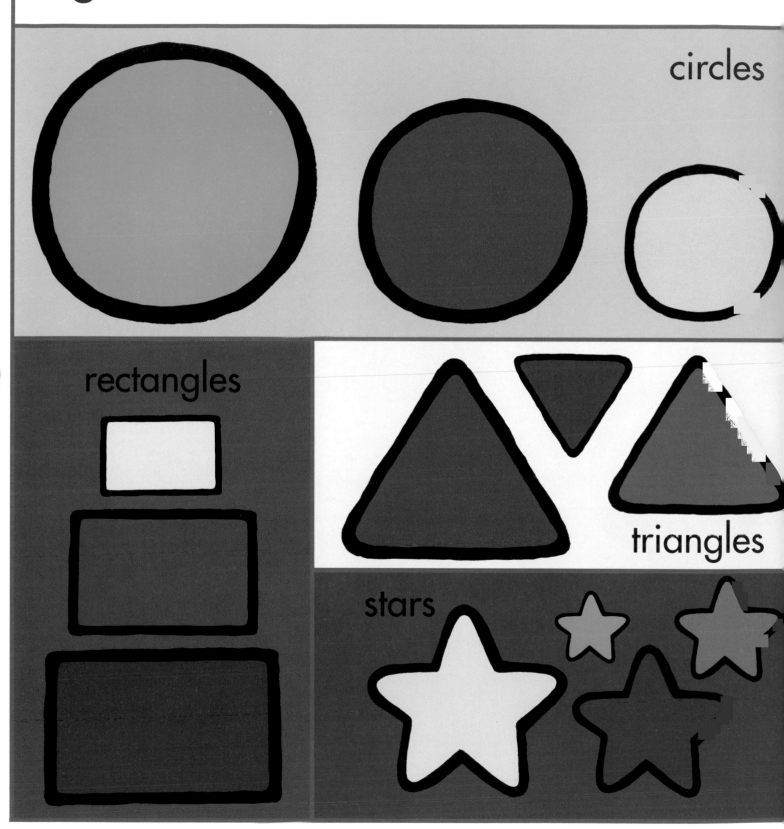

circles

rectangles

triangles

stars

42

Which is the smallest star?

aeroplanes

lorries

motorbikes

roller-skates

Which is the largest motorbike?

Find the shapes at the party

cakes

balloon

drum

hat

What cake shapes are there?

presents

andwiches on a plate

sweets

clown

How many circles can you see on the clown?

Who owns what?

What shape does the boy in the red hat like?

46

eddy bear

socks

mug

hat

ball

toothbrush

How many triangles can you count?

Now I know...